The Good People of Gomorrah

...a Memphis miscellany

edited by Gordon Osing

for St. Luke's Press of Memphis

ST. LUKE'S PRESS, Suite 401, Mid-Memphis Tower,
1407 Union Avenue, Memphis, TN 38104

Copyright© 1979 by St. Luke's Press. All rights reserved.

Printed in U. S. A.
Design by Betty Gilow
Cover drawing by Marvina Wyatt

Library of Congress Cataloging in Publication Data

Main entry under title:

The Good People of Gomorrah . . . a Memphis miscellany.

1. American poetry—Tennessee—Memphis.
I. Osing, Gordon T., 1937-
PS559.M4G6   811'.5'408   78-31841
ISBN 0-918518-13-X pbk.

Editor's Preface

In that Gomorrah of the mind, that lives on, poesy, spirits, privacy, and other delightful offenses of the past have long since given way to various clean, well-lighted public religions, chiefly those of the social order that surrounds us, and the air above the boudoir-and-dining-room town is filled mainly with sunshine and damp weather these days. Darkness drifts out from under the cooling leaves.

And the writers of the town, whose peril it is to work out the splendors and the terrors of secret, luxurious faiths, do so, as it were, on behalf of all. (Peradventure a hundred . . .) They are folks whose paths have crossed in Memphis in recent years, and are displayed here in the order of their birthdates, from Ilene Markell, who is seventeen, to Oliver Pitcher, who, at fifty-four, is the old man of the book.

Thanks are especially due to Phyllis Tickle of St. Luke's Press for determining to publish this collection, and to Etheridge Knight and The Free People's Poetry Workshop for welcoming us into that scene.

The title was suggested to us by Dan Henderson of the Memphis *Commercial Appeal.* We are grateful.

Good citizens of Gomorrah, the authors and I wish to dedicate our book to you. We believe you will find here a strong sense of shared life as well as much pleasure.

G.O.

Acknowledgements

Jackson Baker's "If Thine Eye Offend Thee, Write This Poem" appeared in *Sahara*, "Seeing Light: A Parable" in *Vanderbilt Poetry Review*, and "At the Afternoon Lecture" in *Poetry Newsletter*.

Floyd Collins' "Forecast" first appeared in *Moondance*, "A Last Word" in *Ark River Review*, "The Glass Blower" in *Small Pond*, and "Ghost of the Coal Miner" in *raccoon*.

Marie Connors' "Dover to Calais" appeared in *Squeezebox*, "I Rose" in *Rumors, Dreams and Digressions*.

Dee Fonville's "Drunk Old Woman Walking at Dusk" appeared in *Rumors, Dreams and Digressions*, "Poem to a Musician," "Contractions," and "For a Cat Sleeping" in *Contractions* (Squeezebox Press, 1976), copyright by the author.

Lindsay Hill's "Berry Searching," "Languages," and "Mojave" appeared in *Avilla* (Oyez Press, 1974), copyright by the author.

Etheridge Knight's "He Sees Through Stone" appeared in *Poems from Prison* (Broadside Press, 1968), copyright by the author, "From the Moment" in the *American Poetry Review*, "The Stretching of the Belly" in *South and West*, "A Poem for Third World Brothers," and "For Black Poets Who Think of Suicide" in *Belly Song and Other Poems* (Broadside Press, 1973), copyright by the author.

Alexis Krasilovsky's "Sensational Relatives" appeared in *Southern Exposure*.

Gordon Osing's "My Grandma's Back" appeared in *Cimarron Review*, "The Catfish" in *Poetry Northwest*, "Hoot Owl" in *raccoon*, and "At the School for the Retarded" in *West Coast Poetry Review* and *Three Bk Mk Poets* (Bk Mk Press, 1976), copyright by the author.

William Page's "Less of the Leaf" appeared in *The Chariton Review*, "The Ocean" in *Kansas Quarterly*. "The Rattle" appeared in *Road Apple Review*, "At Rink's Club" in *Southern Poetry Review*, "Cold Night" in *The South Carolina Review*, and were published with "The Red Dress" in *Clutch Plates* (Brandon Press, 1976), copyright by the author.

David Spicer's "Raccoon" and "Blind Man Crossing the Street" appeared in *Uzzano*, and "Raceme" in *Buckle*. "Swans" appeared in *Silent Voices* (Ally Press, 1978).

The Good People of Gomorrah

Contents

Ilene Markell
   13 On Thursday Mildred Smith

Katherine Williams
   14 Summer before the World
   15 Poem for a Truck Driver
   16 Use Me

Amana Ajanaku
   17 Ladies in Waiting
   18 To the Elders
   18 To Our New Beginning
   19 There Was No Pot of Gold

Ron Price
   20 Deeds and Misdeeds
   22 I Never Saw Your Face Again
   23 Standing in the Dark Hall of a Boarding Home, Unlocking the Bedroom Door

Lindsay Hill
   24 Berry Searching
   25 Mojave
   26 Languages

Floyd Collins
   27 The Glassblower
   28 Forecast
   28 A Last Word
   29 Spider
   30 Ghost of the Coal Miner

Harry Bryce
   31 Stand Still Nature, You Are My Make-Me-Do

Levi Frazier, Jr.
   33 Colored People
   35 Contributions

Elizabeth Borroni
- 36 St. Francis
- 37 Forsythia

Marie Connors
- 38 Dover to Calais
- 38 I Rose
- 38 Snapping Cold Celery

Deborah Glass-Frazier
- 39 Where Would I Be
- 40 Sharing
- 40 Black Women

Dee Fonville
- 41 For a Cat Sleeping
- 42 Drunk Old Woman Walking at Dusk
- 42 Poem to a Musician
- 43 Contractions

Charlene Blackburn-Knight
- 44 Poem for a Lover, a Friend, and My Brother
- 45 Green Ribbons in Memory of April Fains

Marjean Patton
- 46 Evening
- 46 Pensacola
- 47 While It Rains

T. T. Roberson
- 48 I Can Not Touch You
- 50 Sunday Morning Rain

Alexis Krasilovsky
- 51 Sensational Relatives

David Spicer
- 54 Raceme
- 55 Raccoon
- 55 Swans
- 56 The Cantaloupes
- 56 Blind Man Crossing the Street
- 57 To Beat the Train

Elizabeth Anne Carroll
- 58 Better than Sandpaper
- 58 Words

Stennis Trueman
- 59 Provincial Mind
- 59 Je Me Souviens

Jin Emerson
- 60 I Watch Your Familiar Motions
- 60 Tall Grasses

Ed Rains
- 61 The Old Men
- 62 Leavetaking
- 63 The Birds
- 63 To Max
- 64 To My Children, Who Will Never Understand

Sara Van Horn
- 65 The Recurring Dream
- 65 As I Dress

Jackson Baker
- 66 If Thine Eye Offend Thee, Write This Poem
- 67 Seeing Light: A Parable
- 68 The Renegade
- 69 At the Afternoon Lecture
- 69 A Party of Two

Gary Martin
- 70 You Are Salt
- 70 To Rosemary
- 70 Grass

Gordon Osing
- 71 Taking a Little Sun
- 72 My Grandma's Back
- 73 The Catfish
- 74 Hoot Owl
- 74 Song of the Scavenger
- 75 At the School for the Retarded

Marilou Bonham Thompson
   76 Last Child

Phyllis Tickle
   76 On a Sunday Morning in the Spring

Edward Blair
   77 Two on Love
   77 Love and the Poet

William Page
   78 The Ocean
   79 The Red Dress
   80 Cold Night
   81 Less of the Leaf
   82 The Rattle
   83 At Rink's Club

Etheridge Knight
   84 He Sees Through Stone
   85 Prison Graveyard
   85 For Black Poets Who Think of Suicide
   86 A Poem for 3rd World Brothers
   87 And, Tell Me, Poet, Can Love Exist in Slavery?
   88 From the Moment
   89 The Stretching of the Belly

Oliver Pitcher
   90 Salute
   91 A Definition
   92 The Kite

Ilene Markell

ON THURSDAY, MILDRED SMITH

On Thursday
Mildred Smith
finished cleaning up the house
early/kids didn't have to be picked up
until three
   she sat down to write her shopping list
   she watched television
   on every channel
   were Chinese
   in gray hats and coats
   sweeping
   sweeping
     snow
she didn't really want to go shopping
   anyway
   sweeping
   sweeping
     Mildred watched
the children got a ride home
   Mildred lost the pen she had been writing with
   she sat and stared
     (sweeping, sweeping)
when the news came on
she made dinner quickly
before Fred came home . . .
     On Friday
she couldn't find her shopping list
so she swept instead

Katherine Williams

SUMMER BEFORE THE WORLD

June is drunk in a Chinese restaurant
    one-third of summer gone
  She watches herself grow
               warmer
                  hot
    and waits for the night
      to end quietly
          in an unfurnished apartment
June is leading us deeper into the desert
    teasing us on
        with tan flesh
           and muscular legs

She throbs to her end—
    oozes over July's fingers
      whispering the plan—
Nothing will change—
      the want

          remains.

Katherine Williams

POEM FOR A TRUCK DRIVER

Someone is driving
   thru the night
      pushing white lines past him
         in the music
An eye that
   moves ahead
      in time to what he hears
         whom he loves
Someone has lost the time
                the ties
                     his mirrors
                       show
                           getting smaller
Someone has his love
   under him
      growling down her spine
         splitting the time
      when she will lead him
      to a door
      and he'll sleep
         next to her stillness
Someone will rise
   to her humming—
      the company
      he can trust
      even though he may not always
      understand her whispering
         before his
               thunder.

Katherine Williams

USE ME

Use me
   because otherwise you may
      never bother to notice
         I'm coming from everywhere
            to see you
               talk to you

Talk to me
   if not of yourself, talk about
      the lines around your grandmother's
         eyes, left from the tapping
            of so many smiles,
               lines that deepened
                  before she died.

Die for me
   because I might kill you
      if I grab too hard
         and it would be easier
            for me to forget you
               knowing I had
                  only been
                     used.

Amana Ajanaku

LADIES IN WAITING

   well, sister
   i'm off
   i'm off
to join the nation
gonna be a fulltime warrior
    but
   before i go
gotta check this game
gotta smoke this joint
   gotta go party
   and
we are ladies in waiting
   while we wait for
     you
   to grow up
   and
   we waited
for another Marcus Garvey
and we waited for another Malcolm
   and we waited
    after
    all
we are the ladies in waiting
   the maids of the world
    while we wait
   for you to come home
from your butler's job
     and
   we have been the
mothers of the universe
the queens of the earth
     while
       we
     wait
     while
       we
     wait
    for you
   to come home

Amana Ajanaku

TO THE ELDERS

    shit
my daddy gave me
    marijuana
  when i was
twelve years old
and if y'all
got a problem
    wid that
y'all can go down
to national cemetery
and dig him up
cause i got a bone
to pick wid him
    too

TO OUR NEW BEGINNING

spring forth my little one
speak new truths
so loudly and softly
that all the world may
hear you
walk proudly my little one
step to the tune of greatness
for greatness is yours

talk clearly my little one
so that all the world may drink
of your wisdom which
will grow as you grow strong
grow strong my little one
be a strong tree
with roots that stretch
into the beginning
of our time

Amana Ajanaku

THERE WAS NO POT OF GOLD

i followed a strange rainbow
it was red, white and blue
sprinkled with red, black and green blood
my acquiescence was not of my own doing
it was force fed to my ancestors
i simply inherited the traits from them
i was taught to be a good negro girl
to straighten my hair, wear makeup
and to go to school
they told me that all good negro girls
shaved their arms and wore brassieres
in the seventh grade, the teacher called all the girls
together into the same room
and had us bow our heads and repeat
the ten commandments and the lord's prayer
she said she was introducing us into womanhood
and when Paula Fay got pregnant
they wouldn't let her come to school no more

on the homefront, they took me golddigging on a
friday at midnight
and when i started laughing cause Lighting
was scared of the graveyard across the field
they told me that i made the gold sink six feet deeper
they made me stay in the house after that
they never did find the gold

after a rainstorm, they told me to look for a
pot of gold
"follow the rainbow," they said
i did
there was no pot of gold

Ron Price

DEEDS AND MISDEEDS

Old woman whose sweeping
and chattering woke me
at two in the morning
on a wind blown night
in late october,

you stand rooted in blacktop
and swirling leaves
swaying with the curlews
in tree branches,

you who own the house next to mine
and the one next to it
and live in both because
I do not know why, because,
as you once explained,
you never live
in both of them, but only
one at a time.

Old woman sweeping the
leaves blowing about in
in tumultuous winds,
in winds thrashing the leaves
about faster
than your broom can sweep
them to the sidewalks,
where you have already filled
a garbage can full,
and still you keep sweeping.

I stand at the front door
listening to your half
garbled chant, listening
to your song to the broom,
or the leaves, or the wind.

How can I
celebrate this madness,
how can I
sing songs that urge people
to leap into life
instead of off bridges,
as I stand and watch you
and listen to your
silly chatter, and know
if I walk out in the
street just now, naked,
my body painted a
deep green, with flames at the tips
of my frizzed hair,
claiming to be Mithra
and singing hymns
to Zoroaster,

you would either motion
to me to go find
another garbage can,
or would be too absorbed
in your leaves to notice.

You would go on
sweeping and speaking
your senseless causerie.

And then I stop watching

and turn back
to my bedroom, and do not think
about why, and do not think,

back to my bed where
I want to sleep, but can
only twist and turn
like the leaves you keep
sweeping all night long.

Ron Price

I NEVER SAW YOUR FACE AGAIN

We seldom had kind words
when in the same room.
Long ago
and for reasons left unexplained

you turned away
to enter the mystery
of a pitch black night,
of a night with no stars,
and a wall slipped between us
the way a quiet shadow
slips across the lawn.
You turned away

and I never saw your face again,

who was once so timid before
your strength, so humbled by your strong
appearance, that I shrunk like a pea
each time you loomed over me,

and your voice like rain, like a hard
rain long overdue,
until the pea's stalk
shot out, up,
over, and around you in a flame
leaving your world in cinders
and you bent and crooked
and me running back,

though I never saw your face again,
back into some vague forest of guilt
back to find the sword I had stolen
from you, to bring it out
glaring in the light and razor sharp

ready to hack off your head.
But you could not wait
and I returned to find you
dancing off into the mystery
that watched you for so long from afar,
skipping off unto that silence,
juggling your head
between two empty vodka bottles.

And I never saw your face again.

STANDING IN THE DARK HALL OF A BOARDING HOME, UNLOCKING THE BEDROOM DOOR

Approaching the door with my keys

I walk a path strangers before have tread
with lesser or with greater direction.

How often have I fumbled with
this same set of keys in this same dark
watching the light peep through the keyhole
framing itself in a question mark;

and after the fumbling, to finally slip the key
into the slot, and lose the question in the darkness

that comes like a whispered answer.

Lindsay Hill

BERRY SEARCHING

Night after night
I walk to the edge
of that tired frontier.

Over the black bridge
beyond the rustling river
to the ghost pool
that fetches no pictures from me.

To that border
of exploded weeds and gods
each year holding its contours
a bit less distinctly.

Nettle memories sting wake
a cup of tea, a pair of eyes,
on the ragged reaches
of a shrinking world.

I startle, verge weary,
between nervous grasses
and that black berried other country
of reflectionless waters,

To think
I could finally step across
quite by accident.

Lindsay Hill

MOJAVE

Pretend you are never
Coming back

The hardened surface
Holds you like a mirror

Heat becomes a kind of
Second self

The silence
At the center of everything

Widens

Now there is nothing
To pull you away

Nothing to remind you
Who you have been

Only a hawk
And the dry hush

Instead of everything that
Owns you

Instead of going out and
Coming in

Instead of chasing
Everyone who leaves you

Tell yourself
You are going out into the morning

With the scorpion
And the hawk

Lindsay Hill

With the wind's
Cloak of sand

Pretend
You are never coming back

Then stop pretending
That you ever can

LANGUAGES

The river
speaks with soft swiftness
a language of directions
it has learned.

The language of rains is different,
and so is the sea's tongue.

The rain rests in itself
saying leave.

The river takes leave of itself
saying return.

The sea returns to itself
saying rest.

These are the languages of water.

Floyd Collins

THE GLASSBLOWER

His contempt for the power
Of mirrors
Grows with age.
He remembers how
When he was a child,
They were still held
To the mouths
Of the dying.

Now on winter nights he sees
His breath rise
Like smoke toward the stars,
And he knows the roads
Will be locked by ice
Before morning.

What little he keeps for himself
Goes into cabinets.
And he has the dream
Every night,
The young girl
Who opens the dark veins
Of her wrists
With a broken angel.

FORECAST

November is the tombstone
At a wheat field's edge.

Now in the shed
Of the casket-maker

There is a harsh joy
In the hammer's rhythms

In the wheezing of an old saw . . .

It is a season
Beyond the simple
Provinces of weather

A premonition
In the golden eye of the crow.

A LAST WORD

The telephone
rings like the blade of an ax
on a honing wheel.
A half-continent away
your tongue shifts
the fine black gravel
in the mouthpiece:
words of stone.

Already it's twilight there.
And in a cold room
with a brush
you strike the last sparks
of the sun
from your hair.

SPIDER

Ruby hourglass
On its belly,
The spider
Weaves with a precision
That is
Swiss.

All night it practices
A crystalline
Geometry

It knows
The shape of
Diamond
And snowflake
Its prisms chandelier the crypt.

A tiny necrologist,
The spider
Has written our
Names like wisps of angel hair

High in the moonlit branches
Of spruce
And fir.

Floyd Collins

GHOST OF THE COAL MINER

All night the whole mountain groans
in a single
splinter
of ancient shaft timber

and come morning
before the cock crows
the miners file
through the narrow streets of the town.

Soon the leaves will fly
and the first flakes will break
into crystal
above the spires of pine
and fir.

Again this winter the bony children
will raise
in some moonlit clearing
a snowman

its gaze black with reproach.

Harry Bryce

STAND STILL NATURE, YOU ARE
MY MAKE-ME-DO

Stand Still Nature You Are
    My Make-Me-Do
Be the African
        Indian
        Asian
        Ebony creation
you are.
Make the vibration waves
that only you can make.
Be what
        Cun-funk-shun
Makes music from
Be
    Conga
    Bongo
    Tamboury

Be a nature
        creation
Since nature is what
        soul inside
        from within
        comin out
        is all about.
Be my inspiration
My nature when
the man thinks
he has destroyed you
taken away my
        Make-Me-Do
Make me dance
Make me paint
Make me poet

Make me make you
on
        onionskin
        brown skin
        soft skin
        skin to skin
Make me breathe your breath
Laugh at the man
through song
                cause
I'm still
        Hangin-in
        Hauntin
        Drawin out
color, warm air,
                Alive.

Levi Frazier, Jr.

COLORED PEOPLE

Colored People — We People
is a hopeful People,

Hopeful that something will happen:

Something good   Something bad

Something   Some change

Something different   Something happy

Something sad   Anything something —
                                  but nothing something.

Hopeful People we are — Colored People:

"Hope you feeling well, Brother!"
                      "Hope you fairing well, daughter!"

"Hope everything turns out all right, son."
                      "Hope you can make it soon, girl."

"Hope your husband ain't at home."
                      "Hope you can come!"

"Hope *you* can come!"
                      "Just hope I can get it up!"

"Hope I can be of help!"
                      "Hope I can help you."

"Hope we can make it, baby."
                      "Hope they don't know."

"I hope the Lawd'll see us through."
"I hope so . . ."

I know so . . . cause we a hoping people;
    and, when we ain't hoping, we wishing or dreaming:

"You know something, I wished I had a million dollars."
    "That so, I dreamt I stole that million dollars."

"Nigguh, I wish you would . . . now I hope I don't have to hit you with this stick."
    "I wish you wouldn't do that."

"I was hoping I wouldn't have to."
    "Good, cause I dreamt I loant you every dime of that million."

Yes suh, we colored people is a hopeful people, dreaming up all kinds of wishes; and if you ask me, I guess that's a whole lot better than stumbling through life just wishing we had the hope to dream with.

Levi Frazier, Jr.

CONTRIBUTIONS

In the rush
to see his blood,
I stepped on his shoes
sliced
like strips of bacon
warm
between the tracks.
"Are these the shoes,"
I thought. "Are these
the relics that lie
in the middle
of the rails,
till the next train passes over,
just like the first.
Shouldn't these soles
be hanging
in some Black Archive for all
children to see
the losses we have suffered."

There is blood on the tracks,
that Bob Dylan will not sing about,
that mothers will point to
and warn their young
arms & legs about;
that David Flemming will remember
as long as he rides by —
head turned
the other way.

Elizabeth Borroni

ST. FRANCIS

For Gary

I never see what you see
but flow the curve of your arm
to wild mystery that swallows
scaled and feathered ones whole
as you trace their secret course
and I strain blind in the wake
of love that cannot blink

until you turn to show me
iridescent knowledge and joy
at the end of all sense,
silver splash in your eye,
mouth hooking after it,
on each outstretched finger
the shine of wings folding.

Elizabeth Borroni

FORSYTHIA

I stood at the corner of the house
to press my face against the cool
of long wood, saddened to think
I would not remember, everything
lost in air, as in high games
of toss and catch at twilight.

For years we play to live,
with return to water so clear
in cupped palms we can see
what fingers close to protect
at sure touch of darkness:

our gleaming fortunes handed us
by familiar children in a ring,
their smooth shoulders bending
over the secret of a bush
that blazes even in the night.

So I am made to remember
the essential white clapboard
and on bright edges of sight
the yellow break of forsythia,
resisting dusk like a child
who hides behind the wellhouse.

I have learned by branchlight
the grass rules, and I swear
by the grain of my own hands
and one house that stands in shade:
the inspired bone flowers.

Marie Connors

DOVER TO CALAIS

The chalk cliffs dis-
appear
and
my luxuries
line up
like deck chairs
on a boat to France.

Newspapers,
Letters,
Books,

We fold everything
with our hands.

This is an orderly
loneliness.

I ROSE

broken with the bulk
of empty buckets
balancing the load
of what you need
from me
which is
nothing.

SNAPPING COLD CELERY

It was
the way
he said
'go on
if you have to'
that sounded
like snapping
cold celery.

Deborah Glass-Frazier

WHERE WOULD I BE

Where would I be
Without that 40-pound shadow
Following me
Everywhere, I turn
Look,
＿＿＿Touch,
＿＿＿＿＿＿Behind.

There she is playing me.

I could be in New York
Trying to be an actress
Or going to grad school
Or just leaving town whenever I felt like it
Party to the max!

But I would still be threading a needle
With the frayed ends of my life.

Deborah Glass-Frazier

SHARING

love is sharing

                    i thought.

but now i know
for you,

                    not only does life

but also love

                    hold no surprises.

maybe the surprise will be in *my* leaving.

BLACK WOMEN

black women
searching,
fearing to reach
to that other short haired
                    black faced
mother/sister/daughter/woman
i know the pain she's going through
i smell it as she lights her cigarette
i see it as she pulls her chair closer to the light.
and her reflection sends out rays to
          every other woman in the place . . .
watching her tears flow as fast and furious
as her man does.

and i turn my head
not to see my reflection
                    in her pain.

Dee Fonville

FOR A CAT SLEEPING

See, I have come

Flesh quivering
like the applause

of leaves, hands
rising up in the sun,

you listen and
shadows in your fur

grow deep, lost
like kneeling

See, I have come

To praise you, to promise
I'll love someone else,

your feet twitch
the skipped rock

sinks by now to the sand
at the bottom

You dream that you move
that you vanish
into each step.

Dee Fonville

DRUNK OLD WOMAN WALKING AT DUSK

Beyond the priscilla
curtains, a
Tree's black claws rise,

Its orange head leans
against an aluminum
building, weeping.

Faces crawl up bus
windows, peer
through dusk,

the moon
will be full
tonight.

POEM TO A MUSICIAN

Even things
having a particular
rhythm sometimes
become deeply involved
with trees
and dogs running up and
down fences
barking
at pedestrians.

    Together
    we locate the
    limb conducting
    when the five
birds
dive past,
turn
as though orchestrated.

Dee Fonville

CONTRACTIONS

The distance between
porch and tricycle
makes a phantom
of her,

the child pedalling
furiously backward.

Your touch approaches,
makes new knots
in my womb, then

rising to check
the clock
inside
the door,

I feel tiny
arms clutching
my thigh, a small
violent face turned
upward whose miniature
thing mocking an angry finger
points the place

and turning back
through the
dream of your body,

I push her out again.

Charlene Blackburn-Knight

POEM FOR A LOVER, A FRIEND, AND MY BROTHER

you cut through the kitchen
brush at my leg or arm
as you walk
like you greet
and dismiss
a pet
after a long day's absence

then, the bathroom door shuts
and the house grows so
quiet
i can hear the match strike

and each time it's done
your voice cracks into song
the door snaps back
and your music spills out
like my heart spills
as my blood sours

and you say,   'it doesn't really matter
              it's not really that important
              it shouldn't really affect me'

so it does
so it does

and no poem can make it better
no poem can keep it separate
no poem/no song/no words
that swing
from love
to rage
and back
can stop the needles that pierce your skin
from leaving their marks on mine

'so it doesn't really matter
 so it's not really that important
 so it shouldn't really affect me'

so it does
so it does.

GREEN RIBBONS/IN MEMORY OF APRIL FAINS

the weekend was just swinging in
hope/hope mixed in the air
with the smell of azaleas
family trying to keep busy
avoid the routines a three year old brings
ignore the empty bed/and
unasked for glasses of juice
forget the tapping
of shoelaces on concrete
but here in the last bit of the month
whose name you carry

April

i will not listen to how they found you
seventeen days later
april/will always remain
warm and brown
singing beneath your blanket of leaves
green ribbons waving in your hair.

Marjean Patton

EVENING

Sitting. Sun going to bed. Moon waking up.
Flies getting off work. Cousin mosquito taking
over their shift. Slapping at your bare skin
chasing the bites. Warm dirt scents and
sweet berry scents drift up on the soft air,
take a seat on the front porch.

Small talk welcome as water. No talk comfortable
as old house shoes. Leaves wave goodbye to the
daylight, beckon the twilight to come closer.
Sitting in evening's lap, resting in twilight's arms.
Day, in its old age, retires.

PENSACOLA

You didn't tell me that once you were gone
I'd start to unravel like a thread pulled from a skein.

You didn't tell me that the string would trail
Between us like a navel cord.

You never said that the line would loop around my neck,
Tug tightly and choke tears from my eyes.

You could have at least warned me about the lonely strain
Of pain that now runs the length of me.

Marjean Patton

WHILE IT RAINS

Come to me before the rain comes.
Be here with me. Watch with me
As the drops collect in specks.
The sound pleck, pleck, plecks.
Protects us from any knock
At the door. The rain cancels
Annoying trips to the store.

Umbrella'd by my roof our love
Will keep safely inside like
An eye snuggling behind a closed lid.
Like that eye, able to see all,
Caring for now to see about
Nothing beyond itself.

T. T. Roberson

I CAN NOT TOUCH YOU

the first time
i saw you
you were a face
on the other side
of a desk
a face i stared at
through a glass wall
of indifference
suspended between us
i could not touch you
your words
strange they sounded
cracked the barrier
between us
as you promised
your presence
in my corner
but still
i could not touch you

you were the voice
on the other end
of the telephone
you listened for hours
you shared my joy
my anguish
you filled my corner
with songs of hope
but no words
no words
could ever make up
the distance between us
i reached out to you
but i could not touch you

you were the body
on the other side
of the bed
you filled my corner
with desires
and pleasures
long to be remembered
you let me make love
to you
but my love
has never given you reason
to stay past the dawn

you have always been
on the other side
the other end
how can i ever touch you
when i know
that at the end
of each day
you will fade into the horizon
emerge on the other side
of the sunset
go down with the sun
into the arms of another
leaving my corner
alone
and empty
and again i can not touch you

T. T. Roberson

SUNDAY MORNING RAIN

sunday morning rain
falling
reminding
me of you
and sunday mornings
spent
oh so long ago
sunday mornings
when rain fell
fell as freely
as our love flowed
and you loved me then
as if tomorrow
were a million
light years away
and me
vibrating beneath you
as the sunday morning rain
beat out love rhythms
on the windowpane
our sounds
filled the empty space
as the swelling sea
rose within us
and burst forth
sending out
silent wetness
to compliment the rain
and now you are gone
leaving the falling rain
to haunt me
as i lay alone
in the void you left
the sunday morning rain
keeps falling
keeps reminding
and i keep remembering
you and sunday mornings
spent
oh so long ago

Alexis Krasilovsky

SENSATIONAL RELATIVES

For my brother, Peter

Last time I left
Bill's Twilight Lounge
with a young black poet
whose words hit home
like the shiny gun
that got him on probation
and my sixteen year old brother
who passed for eighteen
and was fascinated by sensationalism,

we were driving up
to the Lorraine motel
to catch the tail end
of King's commemoration
when the police
shone a flashlight
in our faces.
The poet had left.
My brother, I taught
not to talk back
the way I'm talking now
because there's a time and place
for blah blah blah —
the police said I had thirty days
to get my registration changed
to Tennessee.
I thought about mobility.

My brother thought it was a joke,
something he'd seen on TV —
Beale Street's most celebrated gambler's
reply to the police
when told he had 24 hours
to leave town,
"That's OK —
here's eighteen of them back."
He got in his car,
bags already packed,
and drove straight up Highway 51
into Chicago.

We left for New York the next day.
Tennessee was ablaze
with red-bud trees.
Calves roamed the Virginia fields.
My brother pointed out
farmhouse hex signs,
and my cat watched
New Jersey birds
through the windshield.

We knew we were getting home
when we picked up WLIB
"where the Third World comes
    together,"
and could finally joke
about the Ku Klux Klan
back on prime-time radio
in Memphis.

And then all I remember
is throwing my arms around my mother
and wearing fancy clothes again
and wanting to get married
and pouring white sugar into tea
and promising my grandmother
I'd never change.

The look in my grandmother's eyes,
dying, but sure
she was keeping on through me,
was the same look I saw
on the very next day
on emerging from the subway
into the bright lights of Times Square,
when three white cops
threw a black man
down to the cement,
crowds forming fast
as spittle in their mouths.
One of them
pushed a gun into his back
and he looked at me
and surrendered.

My own sister
must have looked that way
at knifepoint,
demanding forgiveness
while some dude
demanded back
ten dollars
for a blow job
in an alleyway on 42nd Street.
I woke up early this morning
trembling the way she trembled
on the cold Hudson River pier.
I got up and drove towards the Mississippi
flooded with the same tears.

I reached Fayette County,
third poorest county in our country,
and stopped a kid bicycling along the fields.
I asked if he'd heard of John McFerren.
Or the Fayette County Civic & Welfare League?
He looked at this white lady
in a car with California plates
and said Ma'am, he didn't know.
He said Ma'am a hundred times.
I said John McFerren was a hero
I'd read about in a book.
I looked at his face
and hurried home.

Now I'm back
diary and diaphragm in place,
"I Am a Man" sign
hanging on a door,
left over from the sixties.
I'm dealing with the same shit,
like watching Greta Garbo on TV
and thinking I have TB.

It's possible God
kicked his foot into my lungs
the way the white man
beat up John McFerren
for registering to vote
in Fayette County.

But nowhere in Fayette County
did I see the pain.
Only spring
crying out in beauty,
roots pushing through hard soil
people talking through the sunset
about catfish struggling on a line.
Catfish didn't register
to swim this brook.

David Spicer

RACEME

At my mother's boarding house
bright in that dusk years ago
you ambled out past the lean-to
picked up a flour sack
and strutted toward the kitchen
butt wiggling beneath your denim back

Whistling a tune I gradually forgot
I could almost see your French lips
like a runaway valley of lilies
whisper words of pollen
your legs a pair of blue stems
hair petals of the sun

Bending down for clover
you glanced back at me
before you opened the screen door
and flicked a cigarette at the cat
disappearing to Mother cooking cabbage
my eyes lighting the night for the moon.

David Spicer

RACCOON

Speaking with our eyes
in a green darkness
we echoed our desires
listening to the one
we never saw:
*there are thousands
of lost masks
all lost here
and I have been
searching
for the one
with no reflection
but the light of my eyes.*

SWANS

As a stranger wails his first cry
I walk past a lake of swans;
they are my sisters, gentle
ones who cannot speak,
the question marks of beauty:
like clouds following the wind
they nod to their subjects
and glide toward the banks,
opening the gates of the womb
for their white children.

David Spicer

THE CANTALOUPES

She wants them: veined spheres
tumbling toward the tailgate
with every bump of the truck
She thinks of a red light,
when she'll run to the pickup.
She'll walk her fingers
down the rivers of skin
when she reaches home;
she'll halve each one,
watching the golden seeds spill
with the juice onto newspapers,
slice them into sunset canoes,
licking them almost dry,
and bite each one gently until
the seeds and juice lie there,
waiting for hands that never come.
She wants them,
but every light is green.

BLIND MAN CROSSING THE STREET

He waits for moments
fat in a plaid suit
grey eyes nowhere
ears seeing engines
he stands there before
striding in one movement
across the street
like a young girl
in love with herself
blessing the traffic
with his cane.

David Spicer

TO BEAT THE TRAIN

about fifty yards away
bells clack
red lights flash
gates drop down
cars helpless
steel
children
cheer me
at once
i run
bound
to beat the train
a book bag
bouncing
on my back
cars yelling
whistling
vibrations
moving me
faster
hair combed back
by morning
a parachute pulling
me up
a happy blur
across the tracks
still running
glancing back
the heartbeat
of a hundred
with a faint smiling
a miner come home
out of breath
i see the coffins of coal
keep me
from the other side.

Elizabeth Anne Carroll

BETTER THAN SANDPAPER

Sun,
yellowing the room
catches him there
tingling with waking up.
She,
with bathroom coolness,
glances off his sleepy heat.
Warm and cool touch,
shiver away,
briefly keeping their own.
Her body finds no fit
so rasps against uneven places.
Smooth and rough.
Only differences
bring memory of herself.

WORDS
the weapons of liars

the:
        "I love you"
        "trust me"

Cut out your tongue.
What new way will you find to lie?

Stennis Trueman

PROVINCIAL MIND

He shuffled in that way
Of provincial minds
Who think affections
Must be juggled
Through flailing hands
And sickle-sharp elbows.
He could not accept soft words
From other men
And ran from me
Into his own queer world.

JE ME SOUVIENS

Her smile was white, July corn
Full and even and hard shut
Against my dancing tongue.
Her nose was button small —
The kind that keeps a man's
Shirt closed and on his back.
She even had black-licorice hair
That slipped through my hands
As she ran to the door.
But mostly I remember her raucous,
Country laugh and how she brayed
When I wore wool socks to bed.

Jin Emerson

I WATCH YOUR FAMILIAR MOTIONS

I watch your familiar motions:
Your fingers touch the strings
in the hot sun, and the sunlight
changes as it settles on your hair.
The least sway of your shoulder
finds my hands shaping to you again.
I know every line of you
in the way you rest on the earth,
and the now gentle lift of your arm
for her.
I am grown so thin today
that I am fed by sunlight
    caught
        on the edge of your skin.

TALL GRASSES

The tall grasses lean heavy,
with nothing to ease their ripening
under the afternoon sun.
They blaze in the slanting light,
descending to the earth:
   No thick-maned horse
comes grazing here.

Ed Rains

THE OLD MEN

Old men talk about the flame,
the candle,
their hands clean, dry,
like new folding money.

They dream they are drunk.
It scares hell out of them.
But they never tell you about that,
though they think of it on the buses,
on the benches,
their mouths open,
their tongues too soft to push the terror out.

Instead they tell you what will be yours,
what was theirs,
how to take hold,
how at last to pray.

So you give them your hands,
Count their fingers,
Count yours,
Buy a bottle.

When you get home,
you turn out the lights.
You make your bed of dry leaves,
Forget how you feel,
How to count past one.

Ed Rains

LEAVETAKING

This
is for tomorrow
that day
not even the dead
can survive
entirely intact.
And it is for tomorrow's tomorrow
for that day
when life grows so serious
this remarkable little timepiece
of muscle
quits
begins to keep poets' hours
among the seasons.
My friends
the self is rooted
in the body
the body
in the soil
in soil in the stone
the stone
the stone rolls out of existence.
I would have given you a leaf
but the wind took no pity
did not know it was time.

Ed Rains

THE BIRDS

We put our hands away
hid our words
our eyes

followed them.

From the stalkfields
the fencerows
they summoned us

come

you are the ones.

TO MAX

The airedale comes in
shakes my hand
watches the fire with me
awhile

seek seek
he tells me in a low voice

tonight
we will hunt in the same dream.

Ed Rains

TO MY CHILDREN, WHO WILL NEVER UNDERSTAND

With a bent stick
I poke through piles of pecan leaves
Looking for a dead man's testament.

In my pocket
A yellow sheet scrawls and blots
The genealogy of itself.

Dust stirred by wagon wheels
Lies undisturbed in this
The attic of my ancestors.

Under their trees
Always like third-hand clothes
I was conceived in slave quarters.

Sara Van Horn

THE RECURRING DREAM

When my mother saw
That I was making love
To the boy in the road
She lured me to the pit
I don't know if I jumped
Or was pushed
I do remember
Vividly
When I tried to climb out
The vines in my hands
Turned to snakes

AS I DRESS

My breasts
have no meaning.
The chest tans
brown and
gradually fades
into nipple.
The swift
once-over
fondling you
give them and
their emptiness
confirm it.

Jackson Baker

IF THINE EYE OFFEND THEE, WRITE THIS POEM

I live in white space
Nothing on my walls
Nothing indeed in my house
So I draw myself a window
Outside it a Cyclops is sitting
his monsterhood filling up my frame
black mouth gaping for me
dark eye staring at me
All I have to do is shut that eye
All I have to do it with is this pencil
All I have to stop his mouth is this poem
So what I do is
turn and draw another window on another wall
And when the beast
gone mad
runs to bellow at that window too
I turn and draw another
and then another
and yet another
Until my house is gone
And there is no more white space
And the Cyclops and I are the same.

Jackson Baker

SEEING LIGHT: A PARABLE

In the morning, I wake
and turn on a lamp.
My shadow is up on its elbows,
back against the wall, afraid.
I reach for it, and its arms disappear.

In the city, my shadow hides in broken places,
slides into the cracks of sidewalks,
begs at my feet to be let go.

The sun is watching us,
me and my shadow,
There are flashbulb moments
between the branches of trees.
We are seen.
The leaves whisper about it and give us away.

It is late afternoon.
I am lain on yellow ground, burning.
My tongue pants and my shadow
lies stretched between some tall weed and me,
a quivering blade of darkness.
This light will surely kill him.

But it never does, answers the sun.
Only night with its black knife
can take things away.
And suddenly I know —

THE RENEGADE

for Ed Levy

He passed through the woods,
not whistling but imagining
the music of the other side.
Birds called to him, but
the only sounds he heard were
those that got in his way --
the crunch of topsoil, the whispering
of sticks. His feet asked too
many questions. Everywhere he left
a path which summoned him back.

So he took off his boots and socks
and traveled on in silence. The time
to be there was after the last tree —
when he could listen. His feet began
to freeze, though, and with the ice
came a thousand new noises, all falling
from the trees like enormous copper
chimes. A last owl called his name,
but he stayed on the trail until
the spring came,

and another, and another, and then
a summer day when the sun rolled him
out from under his clothes, painted
him through with weeds, and arranged
the gleaming points of his finger-bones
for the next man to follow. The rest
of it, the melody, was in his smile.

Jackson Baker

AT THE AFTERNOON LECTURE

for Stuart Twemlow

The young philosopher
is wearing a green tie, pastel,
a shirt of light stripes,
its pink lines meshing into bars.
He speaks of Kant,
of a dry celery chewed
into the stringy mush of last strands.
"Hold tight," he says,
"Sein und Zeit."
For the modern, nature
has been expunged of Logos,
he says. Nature is body.
The girl in front of me
is body. Her fingers stir
in her hair. She finds a handful,
a long lock, which she peels
away with her free hand
slowly, strand by strand.

A PARTY OF TWO

Long ago, she has called a party,
and this, wherever it is, is always
it. When you enter, if you do, she
will offer you such masks as she has.
Your own face will not do. Nor will
the mirror which you bring. But, once
there, you may not leave unless ejected.
She keeps repeating the words: "Do not
leave me alone in this room." She, too,
is only a guest. Next time you must come
as fire or water. She is a block of stone
this time. You have come as the hammer.

Gary Martin

YOU ARE SALT

You are salt

each time
the same
new pleasure

TO ROSEMARY

listen

the rain
of a coming
season says

softly
your name

and i grow
calm

remembering

GRASS

                the wet
grass
     knows the shape of things
         a while

    knows also to forget

Gordon Osing

TAKING A LITTLE SUN

In the empty center
of the bottom of the hot afternoon
the colorless water of the blue pool
trickles back into itself
the sun remembering herself on my skin:

look around with the eyes closed;
you are seeing in the emerald sea,
in the forbidden room

where winds
can only ripple the color of your eyes

where ghosts pass over
the dark blushing of the other

where you may even gaze
at the father of all brine
something like moonlight here.

If you open your eyes looking aside
you will live for an instant

and be permanently wise.
You may find diamonds
in the caves below the eyes.

Gordon Osing

MY GRANDMA'S BACK

The first time I
by the light of a kerosene lamp
scratched my Grandma's back
with a corncob
from the bushel by the iron stove
in the living room
she said I couldn't do it hard enough
and loosened her coarse dress
so I could make bigger circles.
Thereafter I dreaded being asked
though as I aged
her quiet demand
and my ability to supply
equalized.

I never thought of this scratching
as anything but crude,
impossible to be told even to one who knew her
with her oval face, thick glasses,
grey hair grabbed into a bun,
and the habit of chewing on her tongue.

For gratitude I had sighs and groans,
her pleasure having happened
quite apart from my language.
I was glad I could never see her face.

I always looked with all my might
at the cast iron frills on the stove,
at the scheme in the linoleum,
at the wallpaper,
or as a very last resort
at the curious patterns of white lines
(or even tiny rows of red)
on her back.

Gordon Osing

THE CATFISH

Dusk, the trees and brush around the shore,
the dank air over the pond, hoot-owls,
and unseen jitterings through the shadows
were all around us, cluttered, like a language.
We rowed along the trotline saying nothing.
I reached ahead of the bow to be the first
to the mystery tugging our sunken line.

And see me there, after we'd lifted the thing
fluttering into the boat, noting with the others
the wit of the hook, the torn mouth,
and kneeling in the bottom of the boat
holding with both hands, even leaning on
this two pound cat. It was Europe clutching Asia
in an old Times cartoon.

They talked me out of fearing his dull croaking,
the twitching head and distended fins.
I made him fit my hand and put him head down
into our old blue, speckled coffee pot.
While we rowed toward the car he thrashed and died
ingloriously vertical. By candlelight
I slit him into the spring

and held him up for study, turning him slowly.
He was slipping along the bottom, his whiskers alive,
his eyes as murky as his movements curved.
And he was all sleek, his belly a white sheen,
his head amazed.

Gordon Osing

HOOT OWL

As if you were an uncaused
echo, you ask always the same
question of the evening.
Eyes always at the center of your own night

In the beginning when I stand
in the middle of the sand road past
the home-place
you call in the distant woods
and the evening turns still
darker blue,
as the afternoon hesitates,
the fields growing thicker
around your cry.

In this town, too, tonight you muse
and, city or no city, the mind
circles out.

You are out there somewhere
on the rim of my ears.

Someone inside me opens the eyes still wider and begins
looking for movement in the gone day.

SONG OF THE SCAVENGER

If under the iron, green lids I discover
each time what has always been known,
the beggar is, nevertheless, beneath me, turning
in his dull fingers an old hat of someone's

in merely his latest need. (And the frail rich
able to love only the solitude in things.)
The beggar, who calls even the dogs *Sir!*
stepping menacingly from the shade of the buildings.

In my hands, finally, things have become
what they are. My work is like history itself.
Indeed, I feel like talking a language beyond language.
(For I reject the graceless innocence of the beggar.)

I feel like talking your language. The hot smells
and the rain were not so senseless as his hands
who gives everything away for one, silent question,
who, at best, in his art of asking, almost stands.

Everything comes easily into my song at last.
Imagine that I may be surprised at any time,
that my glance is made solely of innocent complicity,
that grace is the smallest things, and intricate like a cat's
                                        tongue.

AT THE SCHOOL FOR THE RETARDED

Like immigrant dolls
whose eyes are behind scrubbed faces
these five young girls are round old peasant dames
bantering and scolding through the waiting room
in shawls and black coats yet in April.
They have their last age first.

They cross the room
turning and nodding to one another
as if they belonged to an order.
Four keep fists deep in their pockets,
one holds hands with herself.
They've made the beds and scrubbed the floors in D,
and go where they are already
reckoned by patient smiles.

"Soon," he says, "they may handle change in the drugstore.
Later they will take walks in town alone.
Eventually, of course, they will be still
children."

Marilou Thompson

LAST CHILD

How strange your flesh is —
familiar, comforting,
like a thought
I dreamed long ago.
I always knew you'd come;
I felt your spirit quicken
long before your body stirred in mine.
And now I dream
that you will go,
that one day I will hold you
broken to my heart
and enfold you once more
as a thought,
in pain and love.

Phyllis Tickle

ON A SUNDAY MORNING IN THE SPRING

Your father laid you into me with pain —
I still can hear the groan he gave;
But those low moans I made
Before I gave you back to him? . . .
From a joy so like his pain
That I am ashamed
When I remember now.

Edward Blair

TWO ON LOVE

1

Bind me with silk ropes —
I'll spend a winter's bondage;
Chains never bound me.

2

      He
Why may I not, again, nuzzle your breasts?

      She
Because you had to ask.

LOVE AND THE POET

Before you,
the autumn-slaughtered trees,
their crippled branches stripped and spent,
would have been the corpse of summer.

Before you,
the acrid bite of leaf-smoke,
assaulting the innocence of air,
would have choked the hope of breath.

Before you,
the prescient marrow of the bone,
chilled by dank assurances of coming snows,
would have stilled the life of blood.

Before you,
the distant promise of a fecund spring,
the vision, only, of a failing memory,
would have been the absurd proof of Zeno's Law.

Now, after you,
there is no time, no age, no season;
there is only now, robed in saucy green,
bathed in bud-perfume.

Now. Until you go.
And then,
it will be,
once again,
before you.

William Page

THE OCEAN

He wanted me to take him across the river
to buy a gun, as if we didn't all feel pain.
As if his words were the pain.
His jealousy sat like a bullfrog
ready to leap, as if I were a lily pad
floating solely for his disposal.
He tried to replace affection
with silk sheets; suspecting
tenderness for greed, he always
looked beneath the deck
of the simplest pleasure
to find the galley slave
sweating at the oars
imagining a rich captain
somehow sailing at his expense,
forgetting the mutual treachery
of the ocean.

William Page

THE RED DRESS

(Anne Sexton, d. 1974)

Readers in libraries
always look lonely
as if they'd just given away

a gold watch
they hadn't wound
for years.

In their eyes
is a pool
like a deep ring.

What does it mean
when a middle-aged woman's
favorite dress is red?

When she looks out her window
and thinks of autumn leaves
as mounds of death?

Why is she going,
this woman who drives
to a cave,

throws down her purse
and pulls off her dress
like a flame?

William Page

COLD NIGHT

The bankers were dreaming of vaults,
the fire trucks asleep in their stalls
when the cold crept down thru the bones
of our hood and the carburetor died.
We'd thought to make it home
but the gauge was registering wrong.

Keep away Father & neighbors, we're drunk
on a Sailor's gin. Out of cigarettes,
an empty pack of fence posts,
an unwelcoming gravel drive.
The fawn lies in the upholstery
smooth as a young bride.
The armrest hangs out behind
like the paw of a lion.

> While someone's gone for
> gasoline we'll build
> a fire by the gate
> and wait, and wait, and
> wait.

Keep away Father and neighbors,

we're drunk on a Sailor's gin.

> At home the mouse keeps
> its place on the piano and
> the bunny hides in the shade.
> But now I'm drunk on
> a Sailor's gin and morning
> may bring disgrace.

William Page

LESS OF THE LEAF

The wolves of my hands
are hungry. They touch out
to the ivy, forgetting the poison
of the three green thumbs
that stiffen toward the sun.

The real life's not
in the pitched leaf
dividing the rain
or in the blood of the rose
that falls and gathers again
in the grainy face
of the sunflower.

These bones within
the fingers of my hands
I count out like
the creatures of my lawn
into my one long breath
that blooms into
the maze of plants.

If the wind that steps down
into the deepest cave
climbs out again,
shall I this morning,
stepping into the bath
of light, know less
of the leaf and stem
that shade my working hand?

In a garden where I found
my death one morning
in a tangled nest of fur,
from the bed of green phlox
I pulled the flower of my hand
and saw in the vines of my palm
where it all begins and ends.

William Page

THE RATTLE

Is it their love of the dark
that makes us fear them?
Or a memory of an old tale
of gleeless dancers
jerking hideously, until
they broke their limbs?

Once I held a mouse by the
tail in an open field, and
once I dragged a dead rat
on a string as a plaything.

Shall I put on the face of
a cat to avoid any pity?
Is the rattle of a sack
a cause for alarm? What if
compassion's the shape
of an eye, the color
of a rat's stool?

The wedge of bread is laid
on the table, the edge of
the knife shimmers. Precisely
we slice it into squares,
then spread the silver paste,
sprinkle sugar into a sheen;
the brittle joke that will
choke their breath, tarnish their pearl claws
before sunrise.

William Page

AT RINK'S CLUB

Under the dark boards
of the dance floor that
fold the footprints,
the smell of our flesh
has fallen again.

The year the oak tree
wore galls. And you
with your woman-body, your face
already scarred like a storm.
I wasn't exactly disappointed
I didn't have you under the rocking
floor of the dance hall.

But now I must tell you,
stomping the truth
through these thin boards,
"I wish I could dance back
to the step I missed
for us both

and take you
on the hard ground
And then I wouldn't keep
swaying, keep following you."

Etheridge Knight

HE SEES THROUGH STONE

He sees through stone
he has the secret
eyes this old black one
who under prison skies
sits pressed by the sun
against the western wall
his pipe between purple gums

the years fall
like overripe plums
bursting red flesh
on the dark earth

his time is not my time
but I have known him
in a time gone

he led me trembling cold
into the dark forest
taught me the secret rites
to take a woman
to be true to my brothers
to make my spear drink
the blood
of my enemies

now black cats circle him
flash white teeth
snarl at the air
mashing green grass beneath
shining muscles
ears peeling his words
he smiles
he knows
the hunt the enemy
he has the secret eyes
he sees through stone

Etheridge Knight

PRISON GRAVEYARD

The silent shade
from the setting sun
slides over the tiger teeth, lying row
on row beneath the high
and western wall; and tonight as the keeper's
pace cracks the quiet in the flooding moonlight,
the spirits shall rise and fret and fight, because
no hymns were sung to soothe their journey
to eternity, no mourners have stood
in solemn stance and wept, nor do roses rest
beside the teeth. So the spirits dance
the devil's step, and are kept
from the Supreme Justice
of final sleep.

FOR BLACK POETS WHO THINK OF SUICIDE

Black Poets should live — not leap
From steel bridges (Like the white boys do.
Black Poets should *live* — not lay
Their necks on railroad tracks (like the white boys do.
Black Poets should seek — but not search too much
In sweet dark caves, nor hunt for snipe
Down psychic trails (like the white boys do.

For Black Poets belong to Black People. Are
The Flutes of Black Lovers. Are
The Organs of Black Sorrows. Are
The Trumpets of Black Warriors.
Let All Black Poets die as trumpets,
And be buried in the dust of marching feet.

Etheridge Knight

A POEM FOR 3RD WORLD BROTHERS

So keep your bouncing walk, and.
keep your hip and mellow talk. yeah — and
keep your jackknife laughter that shakes the air.
cause white/america would have you move
like cubes. stumbling. without rhythm
or freedom. white/america would design
your dance and your speech by computer —
would have you sit in stiff chairs
and squeeze your knees.
white/america would kill the cat in you.

or they will send their lackeys to kill for them.
and if those negroes fail
white/america will whip out her boss okie doke:
make miss ann lift the hem of her mystic skirt
and flash white thighs in your eyes to blind you
to your own beauty and that of your sisters
who choke back the hurt and hide their love
behind blonde wigs and red wine.
and if you ain't dead
by the time white thighs wrap round your head
white/america will send the thrill of the pill
to kill you.
you diggit? — you diggit?
to down the red devils is to deal in Blk/death
(makes you fuck over your brothers, (cuts you off
from your people, (makes you cop out
and roam single-o thru this graveyard
of white/america. (and your ears will be deaf
to the cries of Blk/children who look to you to
protect them from the white/ghosts.

So keep your bouncing walk. and.
keep your hip and mellow talk. yeah — and
keep your jackknife laughter that shakes the air.
white/america seeks to kill the cat in you
cause white/america knows that fire eyes glow
that Blk/muscles are strong
and that if brothers dance together
freedom won't be long —
you diggit? — you diggit?

Etheridge Knight

AND, TELL ME, POET,
CAN LOVE EXIST IN SLAVERY?

Come then, poet, and sing
To/me a TRUE song.
Of white doves circling
The horizon —
Of guitars/strumming
In the·evening calm.

Shall we/forget, Poet,
The right and wrong
Done, the gushing blood,
The broken bone
Shattering the moon-night,
The exiled son,
The fugitive daughter?

O Poet, your tongue
Is/split, and as still
As the Stone in the Belly
Of The Great Mother
Who/has forever known:
Love and Freedom/are/One.

(All the rest/is/ — at best
A melted ice-cream cone.)

Etheridge Knight

FROM THE MOMENT

(or, Right/at — The Time)

Right/at the time she began to count, —
To compute, her comings:
"Oh, baby, that/was/five."
The world was void, void, void, —
Even her hair caressing my face.

Right/at the time she spoke intel/li/gently,
"Marriage/is/not a union —
It/is a 50-50 proposition."
The world was void, void, void —
And her/words were/as nothing in empty space.

From the moment I felt the bed ashaking,
And saw her breast aheaving, and heard
Her heavy breathing as she stroked
Her pussy and flicked her clit,
The world was void, void, void,
And no/where was/there a light to/be lit.

Right/at the time she whined,
"You spend your/money, and I'll/spend mine —
I'll/even spend the loot from our mutual crime."
The world was void, void, void.
From the moment she flew
Into the warm/blue/arms
of her pistol/packing brothers,
The world was void, void, void.

The music/was/void — with holes in the air,
And our laughter/was/void — falling flat
Against the walls.
And love was void,
And life was void.

And the children of our/love
Will/turn/to pillars of salt —
If we don't walk the same walk —
And talk the same talk,
'Bout being free. *And* thee. And me.

Etheridge Knight

THE STRETCHING OF THE BELLY

for Charlene Blackburn

Marks/of the mother are
Your/self
Stretching
Reaching
For life
For love

Markings are/not to/be mocked
Markings are medicants
Markings/are/signs
Along the hi/way

Scars are/not
Markings scars do/not/come from stars
Or the moon Scars come from wars
From war/men who plunge
Like bayonet into the gut
Or like a black-jack against the skull
Or prick
Like the end of a safety pin

Scars are stripes of slavery
(Check-out my/back)
Not your belly
Which/is bright
And bringing forth
Making/music

Oliver Pitcher

SALUTE

        Murderers
of Emmet Till
I salute you
and the men
who set the
       murderers
free I salute
you. Twice.

I salute
the brothers
of charity
who let Bessie
Smith bleed to
death. She
had the wrong
blood type.
It wasn't white.

     I salute
all self-anointed
       men
who dole out freedoms to other
       men.

I could go on. But won't. I
salute everything, all things
that infect me with this knot
twisted in my subconscious; knot
of automatic distrust, unravelled.
I salute everything, all things
worthy of my confusion, my awe,
my fury, my cursing . . . worthy
of my tears. ALL HONORABLE MEN!
I salute you.

You could go on . . . But won't.

Oliver Pitcher

A DEFINITION

An apartment building superintendent is
a man who maintains order without being a supreme power, with a *carte blanche* to call his
own, a bootblack at the mercy of his polish;
in short, he has neither pot nor window. Bullying, finger-shaking, the power behind the
throne (to himself); everything, even the throne
is a whole size too large yet he lords over all
in his true sovereign, the basement with the
water pipes, the subterranean cosmos.

Victim and witness, vaguely aware of the
form into which he has been hammered, he wears
his ugliness proudly like a horror-helmet,
and tugs at the reins of runaway mops.

At any black as royal hour, just before
the garish dawn, we can hear the endless gramophone record of fanfarannade and abracadabra
of this Minos on a trapeze, coming from the
super's highroad: the basement hell.
  Listen.

Oliver Pitcher

THE KITE

    dangling from a bough-cloud is learned, knows as kin
    the icon faces cracked in Harlem sidewalk squares,
    the blissfully ignorant rope skipping:

        "Lollypop sticks make me sick
        wiggle ana waggle, two four six."

    The car brakes' sudden alarm . . . the kids' unlearned
    hush. So goes the day.

Night. Black

    is the air, white the kin-kite.
    Laborers dream, they do, of swinging at the ball
    and missing in a cosmic Yankee Stadium.
    Swinging, swinging, always missing.

Dawn, Easter parader

    comes wearing a cloche-cloud down to her eyes
    decorated with a victim's shriek.

Sunday

    ah, Sunday, is here.
    Yam skinned women with calloused dreams look
    high, far, to the kite and while wiping away
    Saturday labor beads of sweat, webs of mourner's
    weeping, kindred

Monday

    arrives on the express and waits panting
    at the station.

        "Lollypop sticks make me sick
        wiggle ana waggle, two four six.
        They do."

The kite is learned.

Contributors

Amana Ajanaku (b. 1953) . . . performs social work in Memphis. She writes, "My poetry stems from my experiences within the modern slave conditions in the U.S. . . . I am a Black African American."

Jackson Baker (b. 1939) . . . teaches writing at Memphis State University, where he performs his interests in the consciousness movement, multi-disciplinary learning and pop culture. His poems have appeared in *Southern Poetry Review*, *Sahara*, *River City Review*, *Hiram Poetry Review*, *Vanderbilt Poetry Review*, and *Poetry Miscellany*. He also writes for the *Commercial Appeal* and the *City of Memphis* magazine.

Charlene Blackburn-Knight (b. 1950) . . . works as a nurse and is associated with The Free People's Poetry Workshop. Her work has also appeared in *The Dixie Flyer*.

Ed Blair (b. 1932) . . . works these days in the Development Office of Trinity College, Dublin, writing his poems and enjoying the Celtic twilight.

Elizabeth Borroni (b. 1951) . . . spends her days writing technical prose for a Memphis engineering firm. She has also done some workshop time with new writers for the Tennessee Arts Council.

Harry Bryce (b. 1951) . . . directs The Harry Bryce Dance Theatre. He writes, "I would wish my reader to discover and understand that the Black writer can be as inclusive and eclectic as any with regard to human experience and emotion." His poems have appeared in various anthologies and magazines, including *Poets in a Bottle*, *Regroup*, *Dragon's Roar*, *Northern Lights*, *Go 'Head on Now*, and *Poetry from the Land of the Midnight Sun*.

Elizabeth Anne Carroll (b. 1947) . . . works with the Memphis and Shelby County Public Library.

Floyd Collins (b. 1951) . . . works in Brewster Library at Memphis State University. His poems have appeared in *Moondance*, *Ark River Review*, *Small Pond*, and *raccoon*.

Marie Connors (b. 1950) . . . is an editor for The Center for Southern Folklore. Her work has appeared in *Squeezebox*, *Rumors, Dreams and Digressions*, *Furniture*, and *The Lake Superior Review*.

Jin Emerson (b. 1944) . . . has published poems in *Phoenix* and *Balthus* (Wales).

Dee Fonville (b. 1950) . . . has worked for the Tennessee Arts Council at various times, doing Poetry-in-the-Schools and other community workshops. Her own poems have appeared in *Yes Magazine*, *Rumors, Dreams and Digressions*, and *Squeezebox*. Squeezebox Press (Wichita) published a broadside of her work, *Contractions*, in 1976.

Levi Frazier (b. 1951) . . . works in audio-visual education at State Technical Institute of Memphis. He is also associated with The Beale Street Repertory Theatre. His work has also appeared in *Integrateducation* and the *WBL Magazine*.

Deborah Glass-Frazier (b. 1950) . . . is associated with The Free People's Poetry Workshop. She is presently finishing an advanced degree at Memphis State University.

Lindsay Hill (b. 1952) . . . writes nights and sells municipal bonds through the day. Oyez Press of San Francisco published his volume *Avilla* in 1974.

Etheridge Knight (b. 1928) . . . published *Poems from Prison* in 1968 with Broadside Press (Detroit) and *Belly Song and Other Poems* in 1973, also with Broadside. He organized The Free People's Poetry Workshop in Memphis. His poems have appeared in *Journal of Black Poetry*, *Negro Digest*, *New Letters*, *Black World*, *The Dixie Flyer*, and other magazines and newspapers. They have also been anthologized in *Potere Negro* (Black Power), *For Malcolm X*, *The Norton Anthology*, and *L'Idea degli Antenati* (The Idea of Ancestry), published in Italy.

Alexis Krasilovsky (b. 1948) . . . is now in New York working in film. She was formerly artist-in-residence with The Beale Street Repertory Theatre. Her work has appeared in *Southern Exposure* and other magazines.

Ilene Markell (b. 1961) . . . attends Lausanne School in Memphis, and has published in Andover College's *Thought Prints*. She says she enjoys "freezing experiences into images that seem to fit in a series with everything else in the world."

Gary Martin (b. 1938) . . . now lives in Texas where he also paints and sculpts.

Gordon Osing (b. 1937) . . . has published poems in *Cimarron Review*, *Poetry Northwest*, *West Coast Poetry Review*, *Raven*, *The Chariton Review*, *raccoon* and other magazines. In 1976 he published with Bk Mk Press (Kansas City) a small collection of poems, *Before the Shutter*, in the volume *Three Bk Mk Poets*. He is the editor of the present anthology.

William Page (b. 1929) . . . published *Clutch Plates* in 1976 with Brandon Press (Boston). He teaches writing at Memphis State. His poems have also appeared in *Kansas Quarterly*, *The Chariton Review*, *Road Apple Review*, *Southern Poetry Review*, *South Carolina Review*, *Wisconsin Review*, *Antigonish Review*, *Vanderbilt Poetry Review*, *Falcon* and other magazines.

Marjean Patton (b. 1949) . . . works with the Memphis and Shelby County Public Libraries and is associated with The Free People's Poetry Workshop. She writes, "With my work I want me and the world to see each other."

Oliver Pitcher (b. 1924) . . . appeared in the Canadian anthology *Points of Light.* He has been artist-in-residence with the Beale Street Repertory Company and is a former teacher with the Selma Burke Art Center in Pittsburgh.

Ron Price (b. 1952) . . . is one of the leaders of The Free People's Poetry Workshop, which meets and presents poetry in open environments around the city. He works nights out at Memphis International Airport these days.

Ed Rains (b. 1943) . . . sells Elvis memorabilia and souvenirs.

T. T. Roberson (b. 1949) . . . works in the Memphis Public Schools and with the Free People's Poetry Workshop. She is also in graduate school at Memphis State University.

David Spicer (b. 1948) . . . edits *raccoon*, a Memphis-based journal of poetry and criticism. His own work has appeared in *Uzzano, Buckle, The Green Fuse, Circus Maximus, Road Apple Review, Cedar Rock Quarterly, Poetry Now, Blue Buildings, Silent Voices,* and other magazines. In 1976 he published a chapbook, *The Beasts Remembered*, with Bozart Press.

Marilou Bonham Thompson (b. 1936) . . . is the author of another St. Luke's Press book, *Abiding Appalachia.* Her work has also appeared in *Accent, South and West, Old Hickory Review, The Wheel* and other magazines.

Phyllis Tickle (b. 1934) . . . is managing editor of St. Luke's Press. Her poems have appeared in *Nexus, Kudzu, Old Hickory Review, The Newspaper, Velvet Wings,* and other magazines.

Stennis Trueman (b. 1934) . . . teaches English at Shelby State Community College.

Sara Van Horn (b. 1941) . . . edits *The Dixie Flyer*, a regional newspaper of pop culture and the arts. She has been seen in performances of social satire and skits in New York and Memphis.

Kay Williams (b. 1958) . . . is a junior at the University of Tennessee in Knoxville, where she is studying speech pathology.

Composed and printed at Dave Williams Printing Co., Inc., Memphis, Tennessee, in 10 point Century Schoolbook on 60 pound Hammermill vellum offset and bound at G & L Bindery in Memphis.